T0196171

To Live and to Tell
A Child Soldier Survival

iUniverse books may be ordered through booksellers or by contacting:

iUniverse
1663 Liberty Drive
Bloomington, IN 47403
www.iuniverse.com
1-800-Authors (1-800-288-4677)

ISBN: 978-1-4759-5789-1 (sc)
ISBN: 978-1-4759-5791-4 (e)
ISBN: 978-1-4759-5790-7 (dj)

Library of Congress Control Number: 2012919931

Printed in the United States of America

iUniverse rev. date: 10/24/2012

To Live and to Tell

Child Soldier Survival

Francis Duworko

iUniverse, Inc.
Bloomington

Brief History Of Liberia

Liberia was founded in 1816 as a place of resettlement for freed North American slaves, and became an independent republic in 1847. Between 1847 and 1980, its politics and economics were dominated to a large extent by those settlers and their descendants. Issues of inequitable access and opportunity and outright discrimination became a focus of resentment that came to a head in the 1980 coup d'état led by Sergeant Samuel Doe. His bloody coup was the precursor of a political reign characterized by corruption, violence, and economic decline.

The First Liberian Civil War of 1989-1997 and the fighting that renewed during the (Second Liberian Civil War) Lasting until the peace agreement of 2003, affected every area of Liberia, every village and town, and every family. It was a terrifying experience.

After 46 attempts (political mediation meetings, ceasefire agreements and a dozen failed peace agreements), finally, on August 18, 2003, a Comprehensive Peace Agreement was signed among the warring parties in Ghana under UN auspices, and an interim president was installed. In January 2006, after a hard-fought campaign against a Liberian football star, George Weah, Ellen Johnson Sirleaf took office as Liberia's – and Africa's – first democratically elected female head of state.

Author's Biography

Francis Duworko was born in 1982 in Monrovia, Liberia. Over the years I've gone through tremendous difficult times in becoming who I am today. I was adducted as a child soldier at age 11, and fought for the LURD (Liberian United for Reconciliation and Democracy then call unimo) rebel group in Liberia for two and half years before I escaped to neighbouring Guinea.

By 2003, I became a centre of influence in the Kountaya refugee's camp in Guinea. I founded three leading children/youths organizations that helped identify victims of war(s). Through these organizations, many refugees' needs were met. I came to Canada in 2005 with my half brother and sister and resided in Halifax, NS but later moved to Calgary in May of 2006, where I presently live with my wife and two daughters. I'm so passionate about the future; I don't want anyone to suffer the things that I suffered. I want to make this world a better place for future leaders, especially in third world countries that are still suffering from the paralyzing memories of their past lives. While I don't believe in only giving, I also wish to make a huge difference in the lives of people.

Introduction

"Never let people suffer what you suffered, when you can help them improve their situation" is one of my philosophies in life.

To Live and To Tell is designed to empower adult readers, especially those who have gone through difficult times in life. You are not alone. Be quite assured that I have been there: some were there before me, and many will follow, unless we all work together to find hope and strength in realizing that today is the greatest day of our lives. The most important lesson in life is your perception. The way you see your future, so shall it be. Looking at our present situation, if we think we can change it to a better one, we will. If we think we can't do anything about it, we won't. Either way, we are right; the theory of surviving is about our own perception of life, and how we interpret our present situation will better explain our future. Believe that after reading this book, your life will never be the same. You will become more mature in handling your present difficulties and hardships, and perhaps your future as well.

Remember to always have a goal/dream in life because either we work hard to make our dream come true, or we work harder to make other people's dreams come true. If we consider life to be hard, Life will always be a struggle. But while we struggle to make life happen, if we are actually achieving our proposed dream or goal, how would we feel when this dream or goals come through? Imagine that feelings and celebrations. Achieving our maximum potentials in life is non- negotiable. If you had super powers right now, what is the one thing that you could wish for in life that will make you feel fulfilled? We all have that one dream. Is it attainable? Can we reach it by our own efforts? Can we at least try to achieve it? What do we need to achieve it? These answers and many more will improve our dream world. It is very healthy to sit every day and meditate on our goals and dreams. To be an extraordinary person we need to visualize ourselves doing and achieving great things in our world and then actually doing them in the real world with passion, hope, and faith. This is how we shall accomplish great things in life.

I have always considered today. I don't believe in living in my past. I also don't believe in waiting on tomorrow. I went through many stages of life, and there's not a day of my past that I would relive. I wouldn't be here if I had considered my past at all. I could've been so depressed and troubled to the extent of living in darkness and sorrow, hurts and regrets, pains and frustrations. I refused to impose the weights of my past upon me. We can do it all by ourselves only if we learn to dwell on the end results. It's very peaceful to limit our challenges and problems to today only. We are the makers of our today. We live it because we made it. Everything we do today counts towards who we are and who and want to be.

Acknowledgement

As a child soldier, I was a role model. I was influential. I did great things out of fear that were not done by any of my age group. I gave orders and they were obeyed, maybe fear was the reason for my actions. Later, when in the refugee camp in Guinea, I was a centre of influence for many as well. Through my participation in creating and organizing children/youths groups, many families were fed and clothed, and many more were resettled around the world.

When I came to Canada in July 2005, I limited my ability reaching out to the community that I once served. In 2011, I came across a man whom I had helped four years earlier. This man gave me the courage to write this book. This young homeless man had asked me for change, but I give him hope and a future. I shared my story with him, and told him to wake up and go to work; it wasn't too late. Four years later, this same man who had been hopeless/homeless for two years before meeting me, now worked as a manager at one of the most profitable warehouse plants in Calgary. He is now married with a son, and has a place to call home.

Taking the initiative to write was tough at first, I didn't want to re-open those chapters of my past life. It was painful, but the more I talked about it, the more relieved I became. I remember many nights when I stayed up late, explaining my past life as a child soldier to my wife. I cried out loud and watched her cry with me. I am so ashamed of my past, but I know it was beyond my control. I made up my mind to help prevent children from going through what I and many others went through.

I just want to thank my beautiful wife Victoria for being there when I needed her, for being the better half of me, and guiding me through the written process of this book. Without you I don't know what I would have become. You stood by me when I saw this vision. With you by my side I've lacked nothing. I love you, sweet-heart.

I also want to thank Pastor Berni and Grant Rogers of the WOL Church, Calgary Campus, for helping me start the writing process of this book, and for believing and encouraging me and my family. Thank you

How can I forget Kathleen D Mailer? "The Iron Lady" who developed the system that helped me understand how to put this book together. May God richly bless you

The Disclaimer

All information in this book is the author's story, experiences, opinions and views; any resemblance to others is coincidental. The author speaks from his own experiences; he disclaims any liability, loss or risk incurred by individuals who act on the information contained herein. I believe the advice presented here is sound, but readers cannot hold Francis Duworko responsible for either the actions they take or the results of those actions.

Contents

CHAPTER ONE — A VALLEY OF TEARS.................................1
    SECTION: ABDUCTION   1
    SECTION: CHILDREN ARE NOT SHORT ADULTS   5
    SECTION: LAST ATTACK IN LIBERIA   16

CHAPTER TWO — A STRANGER IN A STRANGE LAND 21
    SECTION: RUNNING FROM THE DEVIL TO THE FIRE 21
    SECTION: START SCHOOL AT SEVENTEEN   26
    SECTION: ADJUSTING TO SCHOO AS A NEW PERSON 27
    SECTION: KNOWING JESUS   30
    SECTION: REARRESTED   33
    SECTION: VOLUNTEERING IN THE CAMP   41
    SECTION: CHILD MOTHER   45

CHAPTER THREE — COMING TO A LAND OF
OPPORTUNITY, CANADA..49
    SECTION: UNPON ARRIVAL IN CANADA   51

CHAPTER FOUR — I WAS ONCE HOMELESS 57
    Statistics of Homelessness in Canada   62
    SECTION: MY ACQUANTINCE WITH A HOMELESS
            MAN   65

CHAPTER FIVE — WOMEN, GREAT MOTHERS 73

CHAPTER SIX — LIVING THE DREAM 81

A Few Steps to Follow During the Writing Process   83
SECTION: WHY CHILD SOLDIER?   101
AFRICAN NATIONS ACTION AGAINST CHILDREN
SOLDIER AND UPDATES.   107
SECTION: LIFE   108

CHAPTER ONE – A VALLEY OF TEARS

SECTION: ABDUCTION

I was abducted as a child soldier when I was 11 years old. I fought not from my own ambition or interest, but entirely out of fear; fear of being killed and the fear of displaying cowardice in the presence of those who abducted me as a child soldier. I was vulnerable and needed help. Instead, I was abused, molested, and tortured. I was told to kill, or I would be killed. I was also told that we were fighting for our freedom. I was reassured that, at the end of the war, everything was going to be fine and good for us all. But as time went by, I saw childhood friends being brutally killed in cold blood and many other innocent people being wounded or massacred in battles. Many young girls were violently gang- raped. When their mothers tried to resist, they were killed. In the world today, some adults cannot be trusted, but the problem is how a child could identify a trustworthy adult. It was a group of adults who recruited me as a child soldier and trained me into a killing machine for weeks, months that turned into two and half years.

As God would have it in 1995, I saw myself in a foreign Country, Guinea, where with the help of non- governmental organizations(NGOs), I was educated and subsequently chose a career to help refugee children recover from the paralyzing past memories of the terrible things which they may have encountered during the war(s). I took it upon myself to be faithful to my new career. Whenever I came across a child who had had some terrible experiences in the civil war (s); like I did, I would lovingly refer them to my psychologist and would attend all the counselling sessions.

Through those sessions, I learned how to efficiently manage my past, and prevent it from interfering with my present or future because I was helping to influence the future of those that I represented. Initially, I thought I could run away from my past, just burry it, and move on, pretending to be who I was not. But the fact is the only way I could live a normal life was by being the voice of those children who weren't being heard, the eyes of those children who had no sight, and the hands of those children who had lost their limbs.

I want to be there for the many children who sadly think it's too late to turn their future around positively. Thousands, if not millions, of children have lost all hope, and are suffering from a total bankruptcy of ambition. For them, all the future holds is doom and gloom. Most of them have been orphaned, and they have consequently taken to the streets against a forlorn backdrop. With heartfelt passion to restore hope and rebuild the future of African children in such desperate situations, I am positive that we can make a huge impact in these war-torn countries by launching organizations that will clearly educate political leaders to the implications and effects of child soldiers after the war is over. Also, those children that have experienced these circumstances can be brought to the reality that life is not that negative. They can still dream and achieve those dreams. The objectives of these organizations should be to identify ex-rape victims, ex- child soldiers, ex-child mothers who try to hide their past experiences and live in fear of the past, and to find positive and durable solutions.

For those children who have not had the opportunity to acquire any form of formal education, we can rebuild their shattered dreams by providing effective counselling and detraumatization opportunities, as well as sending them to school and technical vocational institutions, and providing the necessary medical and other supports that will be required to facilitate the achievement of these objectives.

SECTION: CHILDREN ARE NOT SHORT ADULTS

Children are not short adults as some may think; they are the future generations. We all have the obligation and the power to help them make a better choice with the resources we have today. We could change the future of the world, especially the African nations that are still struggling with poverty, illiteracy, and violence etc. Instead of giving the African children fish whenever they are hungry, let us teach them how to fish so that in due time they will fish for themselves and their families. I know you might not be there to help physically, but with your support in joining the causes in Africa and other third world countries by donating, we will all work together in developing the future leaders of tomorrow.

"But if anyone causes one of these little ones who believe in me to sin, it would be better for him to have a large milestone hung around his neck to be drowned in the depths of the sea" Matthew 18:6

My journey began when I was nine years old. It all started when Samuel K Doe led a coup d'état that overthrew the elected government in 1980, and in 1985 held elections that were widely considered fraudulent. After an unsuccessful coup by a former military leader, previous government minister Charles Taylor invaded the country in December 1989 from neighboring Ivory Coast to start an uprising meant to topple the Doe regime. During the civil war, factions formed around Taylor and those who supported the former soldier with the National Patriotic Front of Liberia, Charles Taylor and Prince Johnson forces took the capital Monrovia in 1990 and executed Doe, while the Armed Forces of Liberia, and the Taylor and Johnson's forces battled for control of Monrovia. From that day, everything went wrong in the country.

I was with my family in our village when we got attacked by strange armed men (Charles Taylor Forces) and since my father was a town chief in Zouglomai Township Bondi Clan at that time, my family became the focus family in the chiefdom. My father was affiliated with the current president, Samuel K Doe government since 1988.

In 1991, when we were attacked, they arrested my father. They tied him up and starting beating him with their gun butts. One of them hit him so hard on his head that I can still remember hearing him hit his head on the living room bench. They also arrested four of my elder brothers, tied them up, and took them away for questioning, so they said. When they had gathered all the villagers at the town square, they said my father was a politician and they were the cause of the war. Some men of my village were among the rebels. When my father saw one of them, he said, "Son, why are you doing this?"

With a deep angry voice he replied, "Shut up!" and shot him in his leg. Later that night, they gathered firewood, set it on fire, and hung my dad face down towards the burning flames. His face turned yellow and then red, and his stomach burst open and his intestines came out, hanging over the flames He was still alive,

7

looking at the crowd. In like manner, my four older brothers were also hung and burned to ashes. During all this, one of the rebels saw me and said, "Here's one of his children," I was devastated and angry, but I didn't want to die like my father. I denied knowing my father.

Sometimes I feel like I don't belong here. I'm as good as dead, I'm not supposed to be here today, but God had a purpose for me: to live and to tell this story as it happened. Making that decision to deny my father and family has taken me to places.

After my father and brothers were killed, they forced us to follow them to Lofada, where they were taking all the hostages. I had no one to turn to. My other family members were displaced. I was confused; everything that was happening to me that day was like a dream that had no end. At this moment, I wish I would've been killed with my family. If you were in my shoes, what would you have done differently? Our homes were burned, and hundreds of other members of my village were also killed, including innocent women and children.

When we came to Lofada, we saw many dead bodies. They quickly gathered young men to bury them. The town was not safe. We had a curfew, sometimes after five pm, and other times way before five. We lived on yams and potatoes. We survived the beating and killing daily by services that we provided to the rebels. The children gathered firewood and the women cook their meal. A few weeks later, my mother's friend, Doumoiwah, who was a business woman, came to Lofada for a business trip and told me the where about of my mother. She then got me a civilian pass and took me to my mother in Lisco.

While in the forest in Lisco with my mother, we heard rumors of children being recruited by the rebel's forces. We thought they were recruiting children around fifteen to seventeen. One evening in 1993, some women came to us in the forest and told us of a family who we knew, were killed by their own ten-year- old son. He was forced at a gun point to kill his entire family, and was abducted as a child soldier. My mother was troubled and frightened. I could tell on her face the fear of the possibility of me being forced at gun point to kill her. She couldn't imagine me killing her, and she couldn't imagine living with the pain and sad memory that her son was killed because he failed to kill his mother. My mother then made the greatest sacrifice a mother could ever make. She packed my bag and a little food and told me to go! With warm tears falling from her eyes, she looked into my eyes and said, "It's going to be ok, just go and never come back. I will be with you wherever you go.

I felt disowned. "I could never kill you, mama. I love you more than anything in this world. Please don't send me away. I can't survive without you, mother, I want to protect and serve you. Please don't do this to me."

She insisted, and wiped her tears. "These men are very wicked. I know you are a good boy, but they could turn you into a bad person.

If I am going to die, it won't be by your hands, so please, just leave; you will be fine."

I had to make the toughest decision of my life. I kissed mama, and hugged her, and started off to an unknown destination. I was walking and looking back, hoping that she would change her mind. My mother and other siblings were waving at me. After a day and night of traveled, I came to Betteba, a small town near Lisco where there were still a hand fold of people living there. I thought I had found a place to call home but in late 1993, we were attacked in Betteba, many people were killed. I was arrested with other children by the rebels. We were severely beaten, tied up with our elbows meeting on the back. They placed our feet between two long iron rods and tied them against our feet. My arm was cut during the beating. We were asked if we knew the people in the crowd, but we all said no. Two of the boys with us were killed, I can't remember why, but they were shot in cold blood in front of us. I wet my pants without noticing it. I thought they were going to kill us because of the terrible things we had heard about them. They later untied us and gave us arms, and told us to follow them. My heart was full of anger, and my eyes with tears. I hated life and had no feelings. I had no choice but to follow them to their headquarters, Vezzalah, then called Combat Camp.

In this town, human skulls were used as dishes and calabashes to drink from. There were no regular cups or dishes. They also ate a certain part of a captured enemy's heart and liver as a ritual. At our initiation we were given these roasted human parts to eat. At first I had a running stomach, diarrhea, but as time went by I got adjusted. We were then taken to a coffee farm that was used for training. They had war casualties. Men, women and children were tied down to coffee trees. They handed you a gun, and told you to pull the trigger blind-folded. Then you opened your eyes and were ordered to shoot another person who was looking straight into your eyes. If you did, they took you away to the next step. If you didn't, you were killed.

Among the thirteen of us, six died during training because they were tired from the beatings and the long days walk. Some of them were wounded and lost a lot of blood. We were forced to smoke gun powder mixed with marijuana and other forms of drugs that they smoked. I had never smoked before, and so it was really hard for me. In the time I spent with them, I never enjoyed smoking, but I did it because I was afraid and didn't want to be noticed among my friends. Then my journey took a different, unexpected direction.

We were promised many things, but they lied to us, they promised me that everything was going to be ok, and they were going to help me find my mother. We were going to be rich after the war. I was one of the few boys who were injected with drugs. I became so high I couldn't feel any pain at all.

I witnessed a lot of massacres: the killing of vulnerable people, pregnant women, and children; and the burning of towns and villages. We traveled on bare feet from west to east and from north to south. Sometimes there was no food to eat or water to drink. Sometimes we traveled for days without any sleep. Whenever we got into ambush, many of my friends were gunned down in cold blood. This struggle continued for days and nights, yet I had no clue whatsoever why we were fighting. Sometimes I asked myself why we killed. The only answer I had was maybe I was just a child and children are not programmed to understand what was going on at the time. Instead, I did what I was told to do. I had no explanation for why we were fighting and for what. Now I know that I was just one of the unfortunate 300,000 child soldiers worldwide at the time.

I had a new title RCO (Regional Commanding Office), and a name changed to Baby Police when I completed my first Gbanga mission. This mission was meant for the brave, they said. When they initially recruited you, this would be your second phase of the initiation process. We went to attack the Charles Taylor forces; to take over his headquarters, to get more arms and ammunition, and to loot properties. These missions were called dangerous missions. It was like a suicide mission. Charles Taylor's forces had different kinds of arms and ammunition, and they had more RPGs than we did. Also, there weren't many of us, and we were not trained. Usually, if you return from a Gbanga's mission, you would be promoted. I completed two missions during the two and half years that I was with the rebels, and was promoted to RCO (Regional Commanding Officer).

All of these things were happening as if I were on a roller coaster. I had no control over things. I couldn't stop doing what I was doing because I didn't have a second thought. This is one of the main reasons why children become the number one destructive weapon a rebel group can ever find. They act on impulse. There is no second thought. Remember when we tell our children not to talk to strangers? We come home one day with a friend, and the friend attempts talking to them. They look into our eyes, and we say it's ok. Then they respond. Well, that is exactly how it is with these children. The order is given, and it's obeyed without question.

SECTION: LAST ATTACK IN LIBERIA

In 1995, we went to attack a market town call Tennebu, Unknowingly to us, the Charles Taylor forces were passing through that town at the same time. Usually when we attack small towns and villages we did all the shootings and killings, but this time around we were being shot at from behind, and we had no chance to escape. Many were killed, including my commander and many of my companions.

I was shot in the forehead, and was in a coma for the whole day. I woke up at sun set. It was like a dream. All I could see was a bright light penetrating through my eye lashes. The blood from my wound had dried on my skin and face. It was like an inexplicable dream of being in heaven, but I felt it would've been a mistake, because I was like the son of the devil himself and I couldn't imagine the possibility of being in heaven. When I stood up, I could see nothing but dead bodies and flies everywhere.

I was so weak and hungry, and felt really cold in my entire body. I was frightened. I was covered in my own blood and the blood of others who were lying beside me.

From a distance I saw a baby feeding from her dead mother's breast. I was shocked and suddenly realized that my entire life had changed at that moment. I knew there was something wrong with that situation. I rushed to pick her up in my arms. She cried out on my bloody chest like she was giving up her last hope and love that a child could ever experience from her dead mother. I took her to the bush. I was confused and stressed over what I was and what I had become. I planned to care and provide for her like a brother, but I couldn't because I was just a child. After a couple of hours she became so weak and tired. I knew she was hungry, but I had no food or water to give her. Then I realized that I was not good enough to be her care taker. I couldn't even cater to my own needs. I went down on my knees, looking up at her face as she lay in my arms, with warm tears pouring down my cheeks. I was so frustrated and disturbed. It was night, and we had no clothes or blankets to cover us, nor food to eat in the middle of the jungle. I know you may not understand this, but picture yourself in the middle of the jungle with a one-year-old baby. She's so weak, tired, and hungry. She can't even tell you what she really wants or needs. I couldn't wait for daybreak. The next day I brought her back to the roadside and sat far away in the bush, hoping someone would come by to help. A few hours later I heard some people coming. I quickly left her on the road and hid, making sure they would care for her. Some women came by, picked her up, gave her some fruit and water, and continued their journey with her and since then I never heard about them. I was frightened and terrified throughout my journey to my unknown destination. At that time I had no idea there were other countries besides Liberia. I knew of overseas, but all I knew was that white people come from there. I had been in school prior to that time, but I had lost the things I had learned. My head was empty. I couldn't even speak English very well, and I didn't care to learn. While in the forest, I lived on ordinary carbohydrate cassavas and other looted food that was rarely found. Sometimes, after days of wandering without food or water, I would come across fruit that I had never seen in my life. Because they smelled nice, I would then take enough, and eat a little bit of it, and wait for a while to see if it had a negative reaction on me before eating the rest. I'm not certain how long my journey took; maybe days, weeks or perhaps months. I can clearly remember one time when I was severely ill and almost died. I was helpless and speechless. I was lying and waiting for death to do his worst. I spent about two evenings lying in the same spot. I wanted to move my legs and hands, but I couldn't. I slept and woke slept and woke until there was a heavy rainfall. Fortunately, it washed me down the hill to an old spot where I found some food (cooked rice and meat left behind by some farmers). I later regained my energy and set out to my unknown destination. I was afraid of being in the open. I traveled for a couple of days until unknowingly to me; I came to Kendu, a Guinean border. I saw an open field across the river, and there was smoke in the field that made me realize that there were people in the field. Because of my fear of meeting people, I decided to return to the forest under an old tree beside the river. I saw four boys dressed like rebels, and they spoke a strange language that I did not comprehend.

CHAPTER TWO – A STRANGER IN A STRANGE LAND

SECTION: RUNNING FROM THE DEVIL TO THE FIRE

As we all crossed the river, there was a sudden flash of lights from all angles of the field which had suddenly become the Guinean Gueckedou border. I was terrified. I quickly knelt down and laid facedown on the ground, covering my ears. I still heard lots of gun shots. The other boys attempted to run, but they were shot in cold blood. I was then arrested by the Guinean soldiers. One of the soldiers kicked me in the stomach and hit me on the head with a gun butt. I became helpless and speechless.

I couldn't even cry because the pain was so severe. They tied me up with my arms behind my back; called (duffer thebe) like tying the wings of a duck. They then put me in the back of their military Jeep and hung me by my hands. The army jeep brought me to the city of Gueckedou, where I was imprisoned for two years.

While in prison, I went through a series of assaults, humiliations, and molestations that I am ashamed to talk about. I was unfortunate to be in that situation at the time, and I'm grateful every day that I'm still alive and doing very well, despite all I went through. I didn't know I was in a different country. I wasn't a criminal. I was a child who had gone through a lot, and needed professional help. I couldn't understand them, and there was no one to complain to. I wasn't strong; I had lost too much weight and was very pale and sick. Despite all this, I was pleased to be imprisoned; not because of the good it offered, but the peace of mind of not having to wander around like a wild animal looking for what I hadn't lost. We were fed daily, and I was able to see the daylight at every morning. Each time I went back in, I couldn't wait until the next morning. I was so excited by my current situation. It had been a long time since I had seen a city so peaceful and full of people. I knew I was in jail, but I had not expected more than what I had. I wouldn't have traded anything for the peace of mind I had in jail. This was because of my past experiences. Few people can imagine what I had been through. Based on my past, there was nothing better. You may begin to wonder, but seriously, in my world at that time, there had been nothing better than the life I was living.

After two years or so, something strange happened again in my life. I was singing a favourite song of my tribe, "Lorma" that caught the attention of one of the new prisoners who were brought in. When he heard the song, he came closer and told me his story. He told me that he is from Liberia but grew up in Guinea. He didn't explain in details what kind of work he was doing then but he told me that

Francis Duworko

he work for a Guinean business man. Few
months before he was put in jail, he started
his own line of business but with his previous
boss's clients, this made his boss mad and
decided to teach him a lesson. He also told
me that his mother was from my ethnic group,
Lorma. Since we had both come a long way
from home, we had a prolonged hug, and I
cried on his shoulder. He comforted me and
assured me that everything was going to be
ok. He was getting out soon, he said, and that
he was going to do all in his power to have me
released too. While in prison, he cared for me
like his brother. He was everything to me in
jail. He spoke their languages and I became
untouchable by the prisoners because he would
talk to them, and they started to befriend me.
The bullying stopped permanently after that.
I didn't believe him at first, but as time went
by, he was released. And I was left all alone
again.

Even though I was still in jail in a strange
land where we had no toilets, and had to deposit
our waste and urine, and eat in the same place

where we slept. I had so much comfort and peace of mind knowing that I was outside of my country, Liberia.

Oh! how can I ever forget the joy and smile that came upon my face. It was like an answer to a prayer from the Lord Himself, although at that time I wasn't yet a Christian. I sat and waited as days became weeks and weeks became months. Then, Shekou, the friend and brother in jail came to bail me out. I couldn't believe I was a free man in a foreign land where I could not understand the languages spoken. I could only see the lips moving with different sounds and effects. I had only one friend and hope, the friend who had given me the freedom that no one else would've given me. I remember following him to his bachelor's home. He opened this huge house and asked me in. "Go on" he said. I can still look back and see his eyes and his smile as he said, "Yes, go ahead." I went in and wanted to sit in the chair, but I smelled badly because it had been very long since I had had a real bath. He showed me my room and the bathroom.

I asked if it was ok for me to take a bath. After taking a bath, he brought me some clean clothes and asked if I wanted to go out and eat. I was afraid. "No", I said.

"It's ok, nothing will happen to you again, I promise it's over as long as I'm alive", he said. I quickly dressed and went out to eat. He was a friend indeed. Day in and day out, he took very good care of me, Money was no problem, and he had a few women coming by once in a while to cook food, do laundry, and clean up. So I became like a prince; I had everything I needed.

SECTION: START SCHOOL AT SEVENTEEN

A few months later, he registered me at Sokoro refugee school in Gueckedou, Guinea. I started school at the age of 17. I was humiliated and laughed at because of my age in grade one with seven year-old children. I was sometimes called names like "grandpa". Every morning before we enter our classes, we would stand in devotion at the front of the school building in lines according to our classes, from the shortest to the tallest. I was the oldest and the tallest, so I always stood at the back. I couldn't understand the announcements during devotion because I couldn't understand English that well in 1997; also, I was standing at the back of the line. I can still remember. Every Monday we had a spelling contest and I always lost. For the first month, I hated school and the people because where I was from we did everything violently, and here it was so different. Then I realized that things were never going to get better than this unless I studied hard to catch up with the class. I started to study very hard, even though I didn't understand what I was studying at first, but I would force myself.

SECTION: ADJUSTING TO SCHOO AS A NEW PERSON

My breakthrough came when the Grammar teacher had given us one hundred words to study over the weekend, from which the spelling contest would come. On my way home, I was reading one word aloud when an old man riding his bicycle suddenly stopped and called me. "Son, what did you say OPOSITE?"

Yes, I said, "It has two Ps". What? I replied" I gently gave him my notebook that was not readable because I had wrecked it while writing in it. He showed me how to spell OPPOSITE, and the teacher had spelled opposite with one P. Because I was new and everyone in the class knew how to spell except me, I used to sit in the back of the class. The following Monday, the first word that the teacher ask us to spell was the word OPPOSITE. No one in the class could spell it except me. I beat the whole class that day, and from then on, things began to change for me.

I also remember one time when I was asked to come and address the class, but I was unable to do so. I was physically beaten every five minutes, and I couldn't say a word because I didn't know what to say. I came first in grade one in my first semester and I was supposed to gave a remark at the closing ceremony; but I couldn't say a word, I knew what to say in my language but I didn't know how to construct it in English. I now ask myself, why did I keep going back every morning, even though I was afraid? I'm still unable to answer that. Maybe I was trained as a child to keep trying, even when it seems impossible. I have lived this example all my life. I'm a person who doesn't give up easily, and it surprises me sometimes. I keep going, even when there is no green light for hope. Had I grown up with my parents, maybe I could have learned a different approach, but I started living on my own when I was eleven years old.

However, in two semesters, I was double promoted to grade six. There were some changes in the school administration that led to the replacement of the principal, Mr. Gbongai. The new principal, Mr. Saliah Kanneh had a chat with me one day about my age and the delay in starting my education. I told him part of my story, and then we became much closer. He used to help me with books and study material, and also offered his weekends to help me study at his residence. Through these private lessons by my principal, I learn English quicker than other students in my school. It also matured me faster than expected because I am a fast learner. He taught me higher grades materials and if I prove to quickly comprehend them, he will give me more advance materials to study.

SECTION: KNOWING JESUS

I became comfortable and began to like school. My school was an elementary school that stops to grade six. The school had a presidential position for grade six students. All candidates were to score eighty percent in the posted exams in English grammar and mathematics to be selected as the president of the school. I was the only student that got a passing mark of eighty three percent and I was selected as the school president that year. After two years of school, I also became a born-again Christian. I became an evangelist for the Church I attended in Guinea: telling people the good news and the hope that the Lord Jesus had brought into my life. I was not yet fluent in English, so the Church had interpreters to translate for me to English and French. My mission was simple:

to show the world His goodness in my life. If I made it, anyone can. I did the (WBS) the World Bible School correspondence courses. I evangelized in the neighboring villages and towns. My goal has always been to bring faith into the lives of many; encouraging them when they are discouraged. Bringing forth the seed of greatness God had planted in them, and assuring them that their best days are still ahead.

My enthusiasm is to inspire and expand visions, so that we can overcome any obstacles in our lives and accomplish our goals. God has new things on His mind for us; God has new seasons for us to come. When we have a heart to love and please God, a heart to live a life of excellent and integrity, a heart to help many people succeed and live with passion, God promises that he will not withhold what He has created us to become, or what we need to become. He has fed and clothed the birds of the field.

Most of us no longer live with passion; we just see the day as it is. We don't like our lives, but we accept it as it is. If we don't like what we are, then we should make a change. If we don't make a change right now, we'll grow old and become unhappy, and that hurts. If we make the changes now and become who we want to be, success will always be beside us.

All of us suffer at times, but history has always proven that depression seasons and recession seasons do cause sufferings, but also serve as a menu for new levels of achievements, inspirations, and creativities that make better lives and better futures. Tough times require faith; big problems precede bigger things to come. If we have never gone through difficult times or failure in our lives, we cannot be successful. To be successful means to be willing to fail in the name of trying to be what we foresee as success. Sometimes we are afraid to fail. That's why we avoid trying, but the problem with avoidance is that success is lying behind it. The more failed attempts we try, the better chances are we will succeed. Life is a risk in general. We have heard of plane crashes, but still we spend our money to get on a plane. We see car accidents every day, and yet we still all drive. If we're afraid to undergo some sort of risk to achieve our dreams, we're already taking a risk by being where we are right now. It's just a matter of time until we realize how scary it is to be where we are right now in our journey to be the person we want to be.

SECTION: REARRESTED

In October of 2000, I was re-arrested, and this time it was for a serious crime. Shekou, my friend and brother who bailed me out of jail about three years previously, was involved in smuggling arms and ammunition to Liberia, in exchange for diamonds and gold, and this time he was killed in a cross-border fight. Unfortunately for me, his identity led the police back to Gueckedou to our residence. Being that I previously had a record as a rebels illegally crossing into another country, I had no time to explain myself as not guilty or even say goodbye to love ones and friends, most especially those of the church and my principal.

Time passed, and time has not erased those horrible feelings. Was I just a fool with a heart so lonely? Who can say why we love those we do? How long does this feeling last? There are those moments when I wonder: had I not experienced those terrible feelings and all the struggles in my life, would I be the man I am today? At that point in my life I was done! I felt that, the God I was working for and praying to have let me down. I started to doubt my faith as a Christian. I even blamed myself for being too talkative for telling my entire story to the whole world. That day I decided not to tell anyone who I was. I also decided that, if I ever had the chance to be free again, I'd change my name from Mayango Tennie to Francis Duworko. I tried holding back those sad memories and tears of the past, looking up to the sky and hoping each sad tear would disappear, but those lonely times and stressful days and nights gave me no hope for the future. I thought of talking to someone, but it didn't seem worth the time. Slowly, hot tears of anger began to flow. The more I tried to remember, the more pain I felt. I tried to prevent those lonely and sad memories of the past from coming back and haunting me.

This time around, I had no chance of being released, coming out because I already had a record of being a rebel. The church couldn't trace me either, because they didn't know where to find me. Despite all their tireless efforts and restless prayers, I stayed in jail, hopeless and frustrated with so many questions that were unanswerable. I had no future and no life except the air that I breathed. I had no trust in anybody, not even myself. While I had been free, I learned that there was another, worse prison in Guinea for real criminals, and I didn't want to be transferred there.

For some reason, I familiarized myself with the wise word of God through his prophet Solomon in Ecclesiastes 3:2, "There is time for everything: a time to sow and a time to reap, a time to be born and a time to die." Through all of this, I was grateful for the daily bread and life I had, and always knew it was going to get better. Hope was what kept me strong and still. I have lived with so much fear, stress, frustration, and agony most of my life, and the thing that amazes me the most is the fact that I'm not the only victim of these circumstances. However, I'm one of those with the courage to speak on behalf of thousands of current child soldiers, ex-child soldiers, victims of abuse, extreme addicts, murder victims, etc who were forcefully initiated into violent situations, conflict/war or crises in their nation(s) or communities. Remember this: becoming an abducted child soldier is like a woman being raped: you're denied your rights and privileges as a person and a member of society. You lose all you ever hoped for: love, the future, trust, peace, and, above all, dignity.

Day by day, I lived on one hand full of rice and a cup of water. Day in and day out, real criminals were put in jail with us, and yet there were others just like me who were caught in the wrong place at the wrong time. One lesson I learned in prison is that; we as human beings can only survive if we think and believe that we can survive. There were prisoners who made it out in body bags because they doubted their survival. Some were wounded when they were put in jail, and they couldn't bear the pain. As for me, I strongly believed with all my soul that I was at a transit waiting for the right time to go home, where I would live happily ever after. These were some positive thoughts running through my mind. Realistically speaking, I had no idea how this was going to happen, but once I believed, it all came to pass and I made it.

This painful stress and maltreatment continued until one morning in December of the year 2000 when the rebels from Liberia attacked Gueckedou, Guinea where I was imprisoned. The rebels from Liberia came in to loot goods and food. Also, it was like revenge because the Guinean soldiers were lunching RPG rackets into the Liberia Foya region where these rebels came from to attack Gueckedougou. It was terrible: the shooting, bombing, people crying and shouting everywhere, Houses and property were destroyed or burned. I wasn't aware of what exactly was happening, but I was taught by the

Church that the world would come to an end soon. I was frightened and confused because I thought that the Lord's second coming was near and it could happen within the wink of an eye. I immediately started praying, asking God to take me along with Him, with my recent struggles and achievements.

One of the main reasons for my story is to empower you, especially those who have gone, or are going through difficult times at this point in their lives, and think that they are alone. I want to assure you that I have been there; some were there before me, and there will be more after you. The most important lesson here is your perception; the way you prophesy your future, so shall it be. Looking at your present situation, if you think you can change it to a better one, you can, and if you think you can't do anything about it you won't. The theory of surviving is all about your own perception of life. How you interpret your present situation will determine your future. I believe that, after reading this book, your life will never be the same. You will be more mature in handling your present difficulties and hardships, if any, and perhaps your future as well.

We were calling for help when suddenly a bomb hit the prison and killed some prisoners. We escaped through a large hole in the wall. I was pale and bony with a bloated stomach. Once again, I was confused, with no idea where to go next. Everyone was running helter-scatter. I managed to follow the multitude out of the city to the nearby refugee camp at Nyeadu, where the UNHCR later relocated me and other refugees to the Kountaya refugee's camp, one of the largest camps in Kissidougou prefecture, Guinea.

I became a normal child again. I became an obedient and hard-working student. I was once a hater of people, but at this time I changed to a lover of people and became an evangelist for the Lord's Church I started sharing my story with the world. Even though our host country Guinea knew that it was not our wish or pleasure to be refugees, they struggled a lot to accommodate us. They gave us back our pride and rights. I started volunteering for NGOs in the camp in their youth activities. Gradually, I later became the youth representative for Save The Children USA and an animator for Enfant refugies du monde (ERM). I then became the voice of the unfortunates who were not heard, the strength of the weak, and the eyes of the blind. War, crises, and sicknesses destroy African children. Fathers are killed and mothers are forced into new marriages, while others are left with no choice but to take to the streets unprotected against chronic diseases, conflict, abuse, torture, mental illness, poverty and many more dangerous situations out there. I was once a child, and these were my experiences, I didn't enjoy parental love, care, or protection. I started living on my own since I was eleven and up till now, I learned the hard way. I know life is a game and everybody is a player, but there must be a winner which means there is also a loser. I was lacking a hero who knew what was coming next, so I could be prepared.

For me hardship is not a threat; it's a stage in life, more or less a transit to a new destination. It doesn't matter whether you have any clue as to the new destination or not. The point is to believe that your current situation can change in the wink of an eye. It's all a matter of time, and time waits for no one I have lost many members of my family: my father, brothers, and even some of my sisters and uncles, but I know I will meet them again, and those who took the lives of my family will be there as well.

SECTION: VOLUNTEERING IN THE CAMP

The new camp I called home was like living in paradise for the first few months. There were non-governmental Organizations (NGOs) catering to the immediate needs of the refugees, especially the newcomers and the needy such as handicapped and malnourished children and pregnant women. At that time in my life, I was made to believe that, despite all I had been through at the hands of the adults in my country, there were still some good people who cared, served, and protected the innocents, especially the children of the world. As for me, maybe there was a reason for me to be alive today, to tell my story to the world at large. I then started controlling my emotions and hiding my past, hoping that I could soon forget.

In 2003, I founded CIA (Community Improvement Association) with ten members. I wrote and directed small plays/dramas about situations/problems affecting the refugee community and joined respective NGOs that worked to resolve or fix those problems, like Save the Children USA, ERM (Enfant refugie du monde), ASPIR (Association of Sports for the Improvement Of Refugees & Returnees), RED CROSS, ARC INTERNATIONAL, GBV (GENDAL BASED VIOLENCE), HIV/ AIDS AWERENESS BRANCH OF ARC INTERNATIONAL, IRC (International Rescue Committee) AND CVT (Centre of Victims of torture). These were a few of the NGOs that were operating in the Kountaya refugee camp, Guinea at the time. After a years serving humanity in the refugee setting, I realized another problem. The children's primary needs were often not met. Various NGOs were busy focusing on issues that directly related to their jobs, instead of focusing on the children's best interests. The problem was, if a child's main problem was hunger, and the NGO worker's major interest was to investigate the child's relocation into the camp, the NGO worker would ignore the hunger and focus on what he/she wanted to hear. This information would be gathered and sent to the UNHCR head office as though everything was ok with that family.

I wrote two new proposals/projects (CPYC) "Child Protection Youth Committee" with Save the Children and (CBC) "Child Broadcasting Committee" with ERM, with the help of UNHCR, in collaboration with the Kissidougou FM radio station. These two proposals were approved for The Voice of The African Child, and were successful. These didn't last long, for I left the following year for Canada.

It was really hard on me at first. When I sent the proposal to the head office for The Voice of The Children to be heard directly, so that the Geneva office could have a chance to hear the long-silenced voices of the refugee children, and they could have that sense of understanding what they were experiencing in the camp, despite Geneva's supervision of the refugee system. A Few weeks later, my proposal was approved and a budget was sent to run the first show. My centre coordinator, Mr. Sandi greedily squandered the money, leaving me with nothing to run the project. I had a presentation to make to the community, and there were no funds left to continue the project. However, I managed with other source of my income to make that first program success.

There were children from many age groups and backgrounds. We heard individual stories about their major concerns in terms of security, shelter, food, and clothing. We also heard poems about their life experiences. My favourite came from Serena, a 15 year-old girl with a magnificent 3-year-old daughter, it went like this:

SECTION: CHILD MOTHER

"Becoming a mother at the age of 13 is my most unfortunate experience as a child and a woman. I was only 11 when I unknowingly became a housewife. I was forced to follow my combatant husband as a cat its tail. I was also forced to be ready to attend to his wicked nature at anytime, anywhere, and anyhow. This was the order of the day. This maltreatment and painful stress continued until I became pregnant. I lived on ordinary carbohydrate cassava and other looted food which was rarely found. I became pale and bony, with a bulging stomach. I wanted to deliver or die. Instead, I sat as warm tears of anger ran down my cheeks. I hated myself for being a woman. My mother was raped and killed by an armed gang of men. Sometimes I was forced to sleep with my combatant husband's Chief of stars, and other important guests. Life was meaningless to me and I believe you're on this journey with me. I had no hope, no friends, no future, no present, and nobody to turn to. I feel ashamed of myself talking to people about this shameful situation, especially being a woman who lost her pride and dignity.

I believe there are women out there just like me who went through circumstances like me, but are afraid or ashamed to share their stories with the world. I think I was destined to be the voice of all struggling women who were or are in crises, conflict, or a war situation. One day I gave birth in the bush with the help of an untrained medical person with an unsterilized knife that was used to slaughter enemies. At the age of 13, I had somebody calling me "mother". This is hopeless, frustrating, and meaningless. Mother; I am a child mother".

I thank God every day for His loving kindness and mercy upon me as a blessed child, and also for my readers. I hope these stores enlighten your mind to reach out to those people in similar situations in under-developed countries that are affected by war or crisis. There were hundreds of people at the ERM Kailondo centre, one of the four centres in the refugee camps at the time. People present were in tears sympathizing with this young lady, and a dozen other stories and experiences that were shared. When I first saw Serena during my activity as a peda-psycho animator dealing with children aged nine to eighteen, she was very excited to be part of the center activities. There was something very unique about her: she was unbreakable. She was the toughest girl at the center. She was outspoken, but she didn't trust anybody. At first, she wouldn't even give you her real name if she was asked. She had a major issue with the centre administration because she gave a new name every day. For some reason, we got along so well. We were like brother and sister. We shared information about our past and present challenges, and where the past was leading us. I tried to encourage her to share some information with the world, in order to relief her mind. She granted me permission to introduce her and her story to the world.

I do pray and hope that children born into different societies and communities across the world will never experience what I and others have. Peaceful countries like Canada, the United States, and other developed countries should be thankful for a system that strives to abolish all sources of corruption that could lead to war or conflict.

Choose carefully the people you want to spend time with. If you need potential to create your reality, you won't need someone else to make you realize how great you are. The result of stress is a terminal illness, but incurable means curable from within. A man becomes what he/she thinks of. War, terrorism, child abuse, corruption, crisis, etc in under-developed nations can be eliminated. Learn to be calm and take your mind off the negative. All the power we have is from inside of us. That means we can control it. To make a quick fix in life is bit by bit, little by little. I am been successful today with a beautiful family to die for, a great community that I am proud of, in a wonderful country, Canada. For those of you looking for a home, may God bless your hearts. My family have found a place to call home: Canada.

CHAPTER THREE - COMING TO A LAND OF OPPORTUNITY, CANADA

My country was afraid of me, and I was intimidated by my past.

My country and community were aware of the fact that I was only eleven when I was abducted as a child soldier to fight a war whose cause I did not know. I was drugged and denied my right as a child; instead I was considered to be a short adult. Yes, I fought a war whose cause I did not know; not from my own ambition or interest, but entirely out of fear: fear of being killed, and fear of showing fear to those who abducted me as a child soldier. I was told to kill. I was told to destroy. I was drugged, abused, molested, and maltreated. As a child soldier, I thought life was so harsh, it hurt. Life with others wouldn't always work. But if loneliness was wrong and togetherness was too, what else was there left for me to do? Suddenly, my country didn't seem so great. I dreamed my life away. Love became hate when I couldn't take the pain anymore. After the Liberian civil war, I tried returning home as others had, but fear wouldn't let me. Even if my community could accept me I would still be a slave to my emotions and the feelings of my past. I was rejected by my community because I was judged by my past as a child soldier. I understood the grievances expressed by my community members, but I hadn't fought out of my own ambitions or interest but out of fear: fear of being killed and fear of showing fear. Now I was being rejected by my friends and community. Everyone was afraid to have anything to do with me except those who didn't know my past.

SECTION: UNPON ARRIVAL
IN CANADA

During my voluntary work involving the refugee camp, I met many great international workers. Among them was a lady named, Esther Dinginman from the United States. We became very good friends. During the years of working with Esther, I built this confidential relationship with her because she was the psychologist that I reported to directly with protection issues. I was a Peda-psychologist, an activity developer with ERM. After developing these activities, they will be designed to help identify children suffering from the symptoms that we were hoping to see in them. Children, most especially those that are victims of circumstances need a confidential relationship. Where, you the adult or the worker gradually nurture that relationship before they could be open to you. These activities were meant to identify such children, note them and refer them to the psychologist, who will then create that opportunity for the kid to enroll appropriate counselling. I had to confide in her for my daily activities with the kids I was working with. I knew she was special. Even though I had already decided to hide my past and pretend to be who I was at that time, I once had a conversation with her that made her really interested in hearing my story. I was afraid to reveal the real me because I didn't want to be rearrested again by the Guinean government, and I didn't know what the implications would be if I told her everything. So I told her part of my story. A few months later, she called me and asked me to write my story down and give it to her. She was going to send it to a third country for me to be resettled and advance my knowledge and security. At that time I thought to myself, I'm not sure what she's about, but I did as she asked me. At this time I was in the process of bring two of my family members from one of the camps in the Macenta region in Guinea. I saw a Red Cross adverts that had the name of my brother and sister. I completed all the paper work as required; a few months later my fifteen year-old half sister and my ten-year old half brother joined me in Kountaya. I was busy with the day to day affairs of my organizations as usual. What I didn't know was that they both had their parents living in the refugee camp where I was living. But due to the time spent apart, it became very impossible for my half sister and brother to be reunited with their mothers. My sister and brother totally had a different approach on life while their parents still thinking that things were like they used to be in Liberia. The parent had wanted total control over their children as usual, but the children had gone through a lot that they could find their own way out without the guardian of the parents. I being who I was at the time I became the only person who understood them and accepted them as they were. This is why they became my dependents.

A few years after she left, I received a call from the UNHCR protection officer. She interviewed me and my family. At this time, the Guinean was placing their family on the resettlement cases leaving the original families behind. For us, after the first interview, it took over one year before I heard from the protection officer. We thought our application had been compromised. The whole process from application to departure was a nightmare. After another two years of paperwork, interviews, and blood work, I and my half sister and brother were resettled in Canada in 2005. This was our first time in an aeroplane; we were rejoicing and celebrating our freedom. We travelled by Air France from Conakry, Guinea to the capital of Mauritania, and continued our flight to Paris, and then to Toronto. Upon arrival in Toronto, we were amazed at all the beautiful sights that were beyond our imagination. We met friendly and supportive people at the Toronto International airport. We didn't know our way around, but they were very kind to us to direct us to our next flight to Halifax, NS.

Upon landing in Halifax, my half brother took ill, and was rushed to the IWK children's hospital in Halifax, NS. After weeks of numerous tests and exams, I was told that my brother had cancer of his spleen, and that he needed blood. His blood was too low for the procedure and chemotherapy treatments that he was going to have. My brother refused a blood transfusion, and I was troubled. I hadn't wanted to lost my brother here, after all that we went through together to get in this land. The treatment took six month living at the hospital before we could move into our own apartment. I had a rough start in Canada, but thank God my brother is cancer-free, and very well today. After a year in Halifax we moved to Calgary for greater opportunity in our lives.

CHAPTER FOUR – I WAS ONCE HOMELESS

Let me tell you something that you don't know about me. I was once homeless in Calgary. It happened when I was working for Warwick industries as a truck driver, and I had a workplace accident in a third-party yard, while unloading my flat deck trailer. I was at the other side of the deck, organizing the stripes that were used to stripe down the bundles that were on the deck in the storage compartment when the forklift operator knocked me down with one of the bundles. I had four skids weighing five hundred pounds each, with a double door frame in the middle. The forklift driver tried to take two skids at a time instead of the normal procedure, one at a time He pushed the other skid off the trailer, and it fell on my side of the deck. In an attempt to escape from the packages, I got struck on my back and felt in the snow on the ground and passed out. Instead of them calling the ambulance, they called my work. My work sent one of their safety workers to come and personally carry me to the hospital for treatment. When he got there about fifteen minutes later, he took me to their company doctor for an alcohol and drug test before being taken in his private vehicle to the Rocky View General Hospital for treatment. He left me with a note to come to work the next day, for some paperwork. I didn't make it to work the next day, but I did call in. After three days on pain meds, I went to work to fill out forms.

Upon my arrival, they told me that everything was going to be ok, but I told them I couldn't work because my doctor prescribed rest. They made me fill out an accident report form, and told me that they were going to investigate. After the investigation, they called me in and fired me with no reason. "You haven't passed the probationary period", they told me. I had just worked there for two months and 23 days. Life became unfair to me again. I had no income and no nothing from WCB (Worker Compensation Board). WCB said they wouldn't pay me because my boss had fired me. No lawyer would help me because I had already signed the WCB paperwork, and I couldn't get any money from my employer for wrongful dismissal because I was still under probation. I was a single father at the time with a girl that I had just adopted about a year ago. I had a very good neighbour that volunteers to look after my newly adopted daughter, Fatu James at the time. I had nowhere to turn to, and I was really sick. My physiotherapy had stopped because I didn't have money to pay for treatments. My landlord took me to court and, after explaining my situation to the judge, the judge advised me to leave the property immediately. I thought I had failed my kid, but I moved in with my brother who already had three boys living with him in a single-bedroom apartment. I had to give away all of our belongings to neighbours because I had no money to store them, and there was no place in my brother's apartment. I spent most nights wandering around waiting for daybreak to start hustling.

After A few weeks, I started looking for a job. I faked my physical ability. I said I could lift 50 lbs, had no health problems, and was physically fit to do the job. I got a job with DIRTT. After one month of work for DIRTT, I had a car accident and my back injury became worse. My doctor gave me two months off work. I immediately took the doctor's note to my work because I didn't want to lose this job again after I recover. When I returned to work after the two months, Unfortunately, Howard, the supervisor at the time, may his soul rest in peace, called me in for a review because it was already three months in total since I had started working with him. He fired me, saying that I didn't make it through probation. I tried to explain my injury and the doctor's note that I had previously given him prior to my two months off work. He told me that he had a multi-million dollar company to run, and if he started listening to individuals' personal problems, there'd be no one to do the job. I got fired again, with no savings or working relatives around to help me. I was devastated.

However, I managed to find another job, and got back on my feet. I was only asked to stop working at the location but I was not told that I couldn't make my dream come through.

I had hope in my future. I knew my life wasn't over yet, because I knew where I had come from, and I also knew where I was going. I was ready every single day to get back on my feet. By the grace of God, within two weeks I got back on my feet again. And since then, I have learnt to have savings for hard time or unforeseen events. I believe with all my heart that anyone of us can fall at any time. There's nothing wrong with that. The challenge is not when we fall, but what should we do next? We should always try to get back on our feet because, while we're down there, people care, and they won't rest until we get up. They struggle a lot to see us through those sad and painful moments in our lives, and therefore they go all out to find durable, yet temporary solutions to keep us hanging in there. Please let us avoid taking the free rides in life. Life is meant to be fulfilled.

Statistics of Homelessness in Canada

According to the statistics, homelessness in Canada has grown in size and complexity in recent years (Wikipedia). While historically known as a crisis only in urban centres such as Toronto, Vancouver, Edmonton, Calgary, and Montreal, the increasing incidence of homelessness in the suburbs is necessitating new services and resources.

The demographic profile of Canada's homeless population is also changing. In the past, men used to comprise the vast majority of homeless persons, now women and children represent the fastest growing subgroup of the homeless population, followed by youth. In recent years, homelessness has become a major political issue in Canada (Wikipedia). While counting the homeless is a politically charged and methodologically contentious issue, the federal estimate of the number of homeless people in Canada was 150,000 in 2005, or about 0.5 per cent of the population. Homeless advocates estimated it to be closer to 300,000 (Wikipedia) Based on the more conservative figure, the annual cost of homelessness in Canada in 2007 was approximately $4.5 to $6 billion in emergency services, community organizations, and non-profits (Wikipedia). While this is a major problem in our country today, I am sure we can change it by first giving the victims the chance to rediscover themselves as who God really wants them to be. They should participate in smaller projects that will yield them the fruit of their own labour. In my next subtitle "My Acquaintance with A Homeless Man," you will realize that this homeless man already had what it takes for him to be who he is today but when I met him, he hadn't activated that part of himself until I sent him to work, and the outcome was unbelievable. This man now has a career, home, son and a beautiful wife. All of this was possible because he took part in a project we planned together. Sometimes it's good to give these people some responsibilities to cater to themselves. I provided the sixty dollars, and he bought the bus pass and dropped off the fifty resumes. As you read this, you might be thinking that it is just him, but I challenge you to try it with a community of your choosing, and you will see a miracle take place in people's lives that you touch. Ever since then, I have been more involved in listening to people's stories and situations than ever before.

There are thousands of people out there who are looking for people like you to talk to and share with. All you need to do to help is to bring yourself to their understanding and listen carefully so that you can identify what their situation is. Sometimes there are hundreds of problem that they may put in front of you, but the reality is, they are saying to you; "what do I do with this situation". There are only a few of those problems they want to address. A good listener has wisdom, and could inspire a troubled heart. There are those causes that we can't help, like job shortages, recession, etc, but I think if we start working on our attitudes towards the people that seem unfortunate and their activities, we could all win this struggle together. Many people have stopped believing they can still make it, and so they have stopped trying.

SECTION: MY ACQUANTINCE WITH A HOMELESS MAN

Here is a clear manifestation of what I want you to know about changing lives. In 2007, I had a chat with a 23- year -old male who was homeless at the time, at the Calgary 4th Ave flyover intersection that changed my entire perspective about the unfortunates on the streets of Canadian cities. Prior to 2007, I was in the habit of ignoring people who go around asking for change. That was until the three life-changing minutes I had at that fourth avenue flyover intersection to downtown Calgary. This man walked up to me and asked for change, with his cap face-up in his hand. Before he approached me, I had already decided in my mind to give him sixty dollars, only if he could promise me one thing,

"What? He said"? I asked him for his name and where he was from.

"Africa," he replied.

"I know, but which part of Africa?"

"Eretria," he replied, with a strange look on his face, watching the other vehicles behind me. I asked him if he had ever worked in Canada.

"I'm actually from Toronto, but I've been here for two years now. I once worked for a company in the southeast industrial park. While going to work every morning, my means of transport, public transit (bus) was always being interrupted by the commercial train that crosses over fifty second streets and Fiftieth Avenue in the southeast. My manager at work thought it was my own negligence to always come to work late. Then he fired me, with no money to pay rent and bills, or to pay my way back to Toronto. I had no place to stay, either. I came here for change to buy food and other stuff, but it's hard sometimes bro".

I was blown away; I couldn't move, even though I had the green light, and the vehicles behind me gently merged into the other lines without comments in that busy traffic. I felt so sorry for his condition, but I knew that he just needed someone to believe in him, and show him that he is the ruler of his world, and he had potential.

"I'm sorry," he said, and tried to walk away,

"No", I said. "Don't be sorry. It could happen to anyone. Here's sixty dollars. Please promise me that you'll buy a bus pass, and then go to the newcomers centre. Print out your resumes and drop off fifty of them before the end of this month, so that you can get back on your feet. We're brothers, and you can't be living like this while I'm doing well for myself. We flew miles to come to this country for something and definitely this is not it."

I strongly encouraged him to live his life to the fullest, because there's no second shot at life. Sometimes if we have a big enough WHY, we can figure out the HOW. We can do anything our hearts desire. We only need to hold the images of what we really want in our minds long enough, and they will begin to emerge, and we'll start to meditate. At that stage, something productive is going to manifest itself, which I call the "creation process"...I told him to go after what he desired. It wasn't too late. If I was driving to and from two jobs, supporting a family of three in Calgary and 11 in Africa at the time, he could do it. He took the money and left. "God bless you," he said.

I drove off with such joy in my mind that I had never felt before. When I arrived home that night, I knelt down and prayed for him and for others I have yet to meet, and decided to keep on giving/helping emotionally, spiritually, and financially. The good thing about helping is that you'll never help others without helping yourself. Ever since then, my family and I have had a great concern for people who have found themselves on the street, due to difficult situations.

In 2011, I was a truck driver for a private business. I went to make a delivery at one of my usual customers, one of the biggest, as a matter of fact. I was on the loading dock when my dispatcher called to inform me about a miss-delivered parcel that was to be picked up that evening. Since I was already there making a delivery, I decided to come in and ask the shipper who was on duty that night. I had an issue with the parcel that was to be picked up, because no one at the shipping desk knew about it except the manager. The receiver quickly called the manager. As the manager approached me, he burst into tears of joy. He called my name. "Francis! Right?" We shook hands and hugged. I was astonished and concerned about what was going on, but I soon realized that maybe he was just being a good manager. He held me by my two shoulders, looked me straight in the eyes, and said, "You don't remember me, do you?"

"No!" I replied. "Have we met somewhere?"

"Yes", he said. "Do you remember some years ago, four years to be precise, you gave a homeless guy sixty dollars to buy bus pass to drop off fifty resumes before the end of that month, and you made him take an oath to God?"

"Uh, hum", I said, just as if I remembered something that happened four years ago. How was I supposed to remember something that happened four years ago? I had wanted to leave as soon as possible. "I was the homeless guy," he said in a soft voice. This was the first place where I dropped off my resume, and they hired me. I worked my way up the ladder to this position over the last four years. I bought a house about a year ago, and got married. We've been back home twice, and just had a bouncing baby boy few months ago. I'm so happy to meet you again. Your encouragement and wise counsel made me feel like I was being spoken to by an angel. I've never forgotten you buddy, and I knew somewhere, some day we would meet. I'd be honoured if you would accept my invitation to a dinner at my house, so I could introduce you to my beautiful wife and son."

"Sure", I repied.

My life has never been the same since I had that dinner. It was to me as fish is to water. I have and I will always cherish the joy of giving to all the causes or needs that I support. Since that day, my entire life hasn't been the same. I feel so powerful and inspired with passion, care to support many. If I had a thousand years to live, I would continue serving humanity, especially the needy and the less privilege. There are many people on the streets just like my friend whose name for certain reason I can't disclose, who need someone to talk to, to share with, to listen to. Just three minutes helped change my good friend. His life was never the same again. We all have dreams from birth, but sometimes hardship deprives us of our dreams, leaving us with frustrations, idleness, guilt, anger, pain etc.

One thing I know for sure is that no condition is permanent, and don't try to make it permanent. Also remember to always seek and you shall find, knock and the door shall be open for you. We're all in this together, and we're all interrelated. We can't make it by ourselves. This is what I would like to say. If you ever need help, ask. There are still good people to talk to, people who care and love you deeply, despite your current dilemma or situations. They are ready to share with you and comfort you in many ways. When you start experiencing loneliness, discomfort, or a lack in any way, try to associate with positive people like religious groups of your faith. If you're not that kind of person, get involved in something like sports or social activities. Never let yourself get down. Try as much as possible to respect yourself because in so doing, others will also respect you. How do you expect other people to respect, love and care for you, if you don't respect, love and care for yourself. For those of us who are prospering, there is a saying that goes; "Those who eat with a spoon should remember those who eat with their hands." Try to be a hero today in somebody's life, and spend some time caring about your community. Be somebody's hero this week or this month or, better yet, this day. I believe that if we all change our perspectives about the people we meet on a daily basis; we could have a positive impact on many lives.

CHAPTER FIVE – WOMEN, GREAT MOTHERS

We praise heroes every day and exalt politicians, and the wealthy but there are those we forget to praise; the women of this world. I prayed for the women everyday; they stand up for what is right hundred percent of the time. They do not run away from responsibilities as some men do, they stand up and face what is right. We have single mothers with one or more children that have taken on the streets as a result of difficulties from their relationships, communities, or maybe their past as a whole.

Some have been abandoned by their baby fathers, husbands, boyfriends and even their community to struggle. Bringing up those kids could be a full time career without salary and taking on these responsibilities as a mother is a tireless efforts that reside in all women as a beautiful gift from God. They stand up and fight for the right of their children; Mothers like my mother Weedor Kona whose blessings has been poured out to many. Mothers like Michelle Obama, great women like her Excellency Ellen Johnson Sirleaf, Fannie Gimeno of ERM Kailondo, Kissidougou, Guinea, Esther Dingeman protection officer of Save the Children Kountaya Camp, Kissidougou, Guinea that I had the chance to work with. Even those that are not mentioned in here are all fearlessly and tirelessly working in the interest of the children of the world. If you divorce your wife, think about the children without the father, who is going to tell them this is right or wrong. If they take on the streets without the mother who is going to train them on what is good or bad. If the children get the right training they deserve, they are going to be the brightest future.

In many prehistoric cultures, women assumed a particular cultural role. In gatherer-hunter societies, women were generally the gatherers of plant foods, small animal foods and fish, while men hunted meat from large animals.

In more recent history, the gender roles of women have changed greatly. Traditionally, middle class women were involved in domestic tasks emphasizing child care. For poorer women, especially working class women, although this often remained an ideal, economic necessity compelled them to seek employment outside the home. The occupations that were available to them were; however, lower in pay than those available to men.

As changes in the labor market for women came about, availability of employment changed from only "dirty", long hour factory jobs to "cleaner", more respectable office jobs where more education was demanded, women's participation in the U.S. labor force rose from 6% in 1900 to 23% in 1923. These shifts in the labor force led to changes in the attitudes of women at work, allowing for the revolution which resulted in women becoming career and education oriented.

Movements advocate equality of opportunity for both sexes and equal rights irrespective of gender. Through a combination of economic changes and the efforts of the feminist movement, in recent decades women in most societies now have access to careers beyond the traditional homemaker.

Although a greater number of women are seeking higher education, salaries are often claimed to be less than those of men. CBS News claims that in the United States women who are ages 30 to 44 and hold a university degree make only 62 percent of what similarly qualified men do a lower rate than in all but three of the 19 countries for which numbers are available. The nations with greater inequity in pay are Germany, New Zealand and Switzerland. However, "A study of the gender wage gap conducted by economist June O' Neill, former director of the Congressional Budget Office, found that women earn 98 percent of what men do when controlled for experience, education, and number of years on the job." A later CBS News article quoted a U.S. Department of Labor study which stated "This study leads to the unambiguous conclusion that the differences in the compensation of men and women are the result of a multitude of factors and that the raw wage gap should not be used as the basis to justify corrective action. Indeed, there may be nothing to correct. The differences in raw wages may be almost entirely the result of the individual choices being made by both male and female workers." In 2011, A Wall Street Journal article by Carrie Lukas stated that: "A study of single, childless urban workers between the ages of 22 and 30 found that women earned 8% more than men."

In the book "Liberian Women Peacemaker" Women are usually seen as victims of wars, as indeed they are. But they are also peacemakers, so that the riches of their land may be invested in their children's education and health services and in agriculture and industry. In this book, Liberian women and men who were caught in the civil war between 1989 and 2003, tell their own stories of assisting the afflicted, feeding the hungry, pleading with trigger-happy young soldiers to stop the killing, seeking to heal trauma, taking to the streets in protest, and storming peace conferences "to speak plainly and forcefully about the destruction of families, communities and the nation." This book celebrates them.

There are many children on the streets of most African, American and Canadian cities that deserve the right to a mother or father and to education, food and shelter but due to crisis and war situations in their community and country their rights are been abuse and these experiences grow with them to adulthood causing our world to go bad, I am not talking about uncontrolled situations, like pre-mature death of a partner but situations we human being can control, such as getting a divorce, having unwanted pregnancy, making wrongful decision for our family etc. Country like Liberia, Sierra Leone, Guinea, Ivory Coast, Sudan, Libya and so many others that have had terrible experiences as a result of conflicts, crisis and war are still suffering from the effects of the past leading their children and youths on the street making the country unsafe for mankind to survive. If there is no immediate intervention our world will soon develop into a land of savage thieves, cruel leaders who will play corrupt roles in our society. I think it is hard time we started paying close attention on what and how we want our world to look like in the future and the better way to do this is by paying close attention on our children and what we want them to be. Every child should have equal opportunity in life despite their physical, emotional, cultural, ethnic, status or financial background. If this is true for all children, what will life been for a child that have missed out on all of these rights and has grown with so much hatred, anger and pain as an ex-child soldier in this world without help will tend to be. I also pray for our planet to keep bringing fort great mothers that will continue making this world a better place to live by standing and fighting for the rights of their children.

Many people do struggle with the reality that yesterday is gone by and that we are not to worry about it because all it has to offer us is pains, frustrations, hurts, disappointments, regrets, discomforts, unhappiness, etc. If you are always trying to make it up for yesterday today, I want you to know that you are in the revolving mode, this is waste of time, and if you are a person that is always looking forward to tomorrow by doing the best you can today, you are in the proactive mode, and this is the mode you want to be in because yesterday is gone and we have no control over tomorrow that leaves us with today.

CHAPTER SIX – LIVING THE DREAM

But something else happened. My past led me to the man I am today, and this is the secret ingredients that I want you to understand.

This is the secret for the many who have, or are going through a stressful stage of life, and feel like it's all over. Be assured today that you will find love and peace. You see, life can be anything one desires, only dwell always on the end results. We all don't want the same thing in life; in other words we have different dreams of what we want to become. We shouldn't get lost in the process or the how. Always start with what we are grateful for. Feel the gratitude, and those feelings will be an opened door to the world; you will be whatever you think of becoming. There are three steps in keeping faith with what you want in life.

1. State It in Writing

Write down what you want in life. It could be freedom, family, love, and peace of mind, wisdom, knowledge, money, or something else. Once you start the writing process, you have actually engaged your mind to work. Everything thereafter that you do or say shall be taking you closer to your written dreams.

Taking the first initiative to write what you really want out of life not only clears the picture in your mind, but it also helps you be rid of all the garbage in your mind that holds you back from achieving your dreams. Research states that humans have at least fifty thousand thoughts a day, both good and bad. If you find the time to write your dreams down, it will improve your sub-conscious mind to focus more on the positive thoughts pertaining to your dreams, aspirations; and everything that comes your way after that will be in line with your dream.

Here is the challenge however. Most people just want to think about their big dream and they think that is ok. The truth of the matter is that it's not ok because that's not how it works. Many successful people I've met have written a daily agenda. Most unsuccessful people I've met have no daily agenda. Your progress in life is determined by your daily timer. If you're a nobody who wants to be somebody, you have to start to think and live like somebody. The writing process is the most challenging part of this exercise, but once you start writing down what you really want, you can have the power to empty a lot of unnecessary negative thoughts in your mind and focus on the dream.

A Few Steps to Follow During the Writing Process

1. Sit, think, and write down the first time you became a dreamer; the thing you dreamed of becoming when you were a child. (At what age did you start

remembering those things?) Also, list the things that were done by others that you admire the most; like doctors, dentists, salesperson, etc. (We're all called to duty in life, but when life happens we tend to shift with the current reality and forget what we are here for. The challenge within this situation is that we never look back to start all over again, even when we feel that it's not working. We then start living in regrets, fears, pains, hurts, frustrations, condemnations, prosecutions and, of course, depressions. This is the case with many of us today. To address these challenges in our own life is as easy as 1, 2, and 3. Following these outlines will not only set you free, but will also improve your daily productivity as a whole.

A. State at what age you first thought of who you wanted to be in life? (your dream) Sometimes the age when we first dreamed matters. For example, if I were just five and dreamed of being a great father and started following the lead of my dad and other great fathers to date, I could end up being the father of this nation, because as we grow, our original dreams are supposed to grow with us. If we lose track, unless we acknowledge that fact and fix it, we will always be regular people. It's good sometimes to sit down and think about our dreams, and what we would like to achieve through them.

B. Did you ever develop a desire to be something else? (Another dream) As we grow older, our desires change with our environments, cultures, ethnicity, geography, race, sex, color, economic etc. This is one of the main areas I would like you to work on first and foremost. When you dream, it's free; it doesn't cost a dime to dream. Therefore, no circumstances should determine how you dream. Again, there is absolutely no method, because when you engage in a method process, you will prematurely kill your dreams. There have always been challenges. Failing is not the question. Rather, the question is what do you want to be in life? We will deal with the how and when and all that other stuff, but when engaging in the declaration process, there is absolutely no HOW question to ask.

C. Why did we change our dreams? (Was it lack of money, educational background, or something else?) Well, there could be many reasons to change our initial dream, but the question is, is there still a need for our dream today? When we face temptations in life, it's ok to battle them with a positive attitude. In so doing we prioritize our life, including our dreams and adventures. But we could always look back at them and bring them to reality again despite the breakthrough. If we had financial difficulty to pursue our dream five years ago, is there still a financial need to proceed today? Will we ever in our lifetime fight to achieve our dream? Will doing what we do today make us achieve our dream?

Are you achieving your chosen dream now? Are you still a believer? (Dreamers die but dreams never die.) Each day is a gift, and not a given right. Leave your fears behind and don't take a free ride in your life. Time is ticking, and every second counts because there's no second try; you live life but once. If you're not achieving your dream, you have to start the declaration process, and take a look at what you're doing, visit your dream, and start working on it again. As I said before, the process is a protocol that we all need to go through, just like graduating from high school. We all have to go to high school. It doesn't matter how long before you achieve your dream, because whether you do it or not, the time is ticking and you have no control over the day and night. However, we can prioritize your day to reach a maximum result. Why do you think we all have the same twenty- four hours a day? Some people succeed and some don't? Well, prioritization is the key; you need to find time: set deadlines to do certain things in life.

I have always dreamed of making a difference in the lives of many, but I was a truck driver and a warehouse worker for years. When I started implementing the declaration process, I began to put the puzzle together. Have you decided to visit your past? Maybe you could get a clear shot at it this time. Visiting the past and starting all over again is a very great challenge, but it's not a sin, as many may think. The past holds fear. We don't want to fail, because it's ok to be where we are, instead of starting something new that we're not used to. So we sometimes say it's ok. Don't ask for more. Don't do more. Don't get more. Don't be more. Let's just manage it, this is life. The problem with this attitude is that, if we continue to be the person we are today and neglect our dream, we will continue to live in insecurity, because we will keep reminding ourselves that we are supposed to achieve more than what we are doing at this moment. If we neglect our future today, we will end up with terminal disappointment. When we are disappointed in ourselves, this is terminal disappointment. If we get discouraged with ourselves, it will take forever for us to be uplifted again. Too often, we get stuck with our present situation, and judge our lives by it. Our present situation is a transit point in our lives. Our final destination awaits us, and, believe it or not, it's only a few miles away from where we are right now in our journey.

2. Believe, It's Achievable by Effort

Believe that it's being done for us. Visualize yourself having and living it in abundance, and enjoying the experiences that come with the realization of your dreams, and set our mind to get it. The strength of this session will change the way you think and the way you act. As a matter of fact, the only reason why people are either successful or unsuccessful is the believing process. Even if you have a dream and write it down with all the great ideas in the first session, but you don't believe in what you've written and act on it, you will definitely fail to prosper. Successful people ahead to their goals; while unsuccessful people look to where they've been. The believing process will keep you moving forward. You don't want to take this step lightly, because it will affect your life.

When we believe without a doubt that God is in control of our situation, we can actually go days and nights without food, shelter, or clothing and still live with peace in our heart, keeping faith that we are definitely going to break through one day. In the same way, if we believe our dreams, things may not always be as we want them to be, but we will persevere until the end. Another thing I want you to note is that most of us have dreams that are not in compliance with who we are. If we don't like music and our dream is to become a dancer, the truth is its going to take us awhile to attract people to like us. People win with people; we are all inter-related in one way or the other. Have you ever wondered why people live together on one small piece of land, when they could live all over the country?

Believe that our dreams are achievable

and that we can achieve them with hard work and concentration. Everything we do in life is as a result of self-discipline. We need to learn how to say no or yes to things that mean something in our lives. If we do, we can choose to believe. A great example of the believing process is the Christian faith. Christians believe so strongly that even if they didn't get what they asked for last night, their prayers were still answered somehow, and they live and celebrate that. Some Christians get sick and pray for supernatural healing or a miracle, but even if they're never healed, still they count it joyful, and live in total peace and comfort. If we believe in our dreams, no circumstances will shift us away from them. Even when things seem too difficult, we will bear through tough times, failures, disappointments, and deceits until we achieve the promises of our dreams. Sometimes it's just the next step we need to take in life to achieve our dreams; other time it's a couple more giant steps that need to be taken.

There was once a newly married couple who planned to spend all their savings on their honeymoon. They didn't settle for less. Instead, they went online and booked two first-class flight tickets and booked the most expensive honeymoon suite in the Bahamas, one of the hottest spots on the face of this planet. In the photos online, the room that they had booked had everything they had dreamed of in a honeymoon suite: hot tub, a large space, and well-furnished to their taste. When the time finally arrived, they boarded the plane for a wonderful start to their new life together. While traveling in the plane, the wife suggested to the husband that the first thing that they should do upon arrival is to take a hot bath in the hot tub, and they both laughed. Of course, it was the first thing to do. When they arrived at the airport, there was a limousine awaiting them for the hotel with a VIP treatment and red carpet. As they arrived at the hotel, the receptionist warmly welcomed them with a big smile, and handed them the keys. "Second floor on the right", she said. They looked into each other's eyes and smiled. They took the elevator up to the second floor. As they opened the door, they saw a piece of furniture, a sofa, a fireplace, and a seventeen-inch TV on the top of a small dresser. On the other side of the room was a closet beside a half bathroom. With regrets and frustration, the husband sat on the sofa. "I'm not moving an inch from here. I'm so tired I don't even want to think about it tonight. Maybe we'll deal with these people tomorrow." The wife was so upset, that she decided to go downstairs and confront the hotel staff. She then decided too to wait for the morning, when they could ask for a refund of their money in order to find some place more pleasant. In life, many of us are right besides our dreams. We just need to look a little farther to figure out that one more step we need to take. As day broke, they both went downstairs.

"What is this? What kind of room did you people give us? This is not the room we paid for on the internet. What's going on?"

The receptionist was confused. "What do you mean? She asked.

"The room that you gave us is not the same as we saw online. We want to leave for another hotel in town."

"Did you open the other door beside the closet?" the receptionist asked.

"No," they both replied. Quickly, they both returned upstairs. When they opened the door beside the closet, they found their dream honeymoon suite.

At certain times in life, we just need to search a little more, do a little more, and persevere a little more. This couple did all the right things, but they spent a sleepless night at the gate of their dream suite. All the frustrations, pains, disappointments, and complaints could have been avoided had they kept looking around to identify the room that they booked online. This is what we sometimes do when we feel depressed and tired of trying to achieve success. We quickly give up right before the breakthrough. Hold on to your dreams, always remembers that when they seem impossible, the battle line is just a few more steps ahead. Keep trying, and you'll make it to the finish line.

3. Receive, Start living it

Be in agreement with what you're asking for, and feel the joy and changes it will bring to your life. Here is the challenge. Most people don't think about their dreams. Instead, they think of their problems, and remind themselves over and over of their failure in life. They tend to blame others who were involved or weren't there, said something or didn't say anything, did something, or didn't do anything, or even those who were not there to say or do anything. Most people feel stuck with their current reality. That's not who we are, that's merely where we are this minute. Things could change quickly. If you think that you're a jerk or loser because you didn't make the right decision to make enough money last month to pay the bills, let me ask you a question. If you received a hundred thousand dollars cheque to pay your bills today, would that put a smile on your face? Well, start thinking about what to do to get the hundred thousand dollars by keeping that same smile on your face every day. Imagine what you really want, come out of that imagination and start to be grateful for those things. Whenever you have a thought, act on it. Don't wait or delay because waiting will have you thinking of the cost that has to be paid and the process it will take you to achieve it. The how, what, when, and where will create negative feelings like fear, doubt, anxiety, and lack. Visualize, because when you visualize, you materialize. Dwell only on the end results. Success is a mindset, and life is meant to be in abundance in all areas: love, happiness, care/support, wealth etc. Strive for happiness first, and all the other things will fall into place.

How can we get along with us if we can't get along with ourselves? How can others love us if we don't love ourselves? The only thing that stands between a person and what he or she desires in life is the will to try, and the faith to believe it's possible. The key to this is perseverance. Perseverance is not a long race; it's a short race, one step at a time. Kindness is one of the most wonderful gifts from God to man. We can never help others without helping ourselves first. Belief rules enthusiasm and enthusiasm exalts passion. Passion lights up our soul and our soul fires up our spirit. Having a clearly-defined goal can capture the imagination and inspire passion.

Prepare your mind to receive what you're dreaming. Sometimes we dream and don't achieve it, because we do not receive it. It shows up in many ways, but we don't allow our mind to receive it. If we want to make a positive life, we must start being and living positively in our community. If we want to be a success, we have to start hanging out with successful people, and quit hanging out with losers. The saying is true: birds of the same feather flock together. Show me your friends, and I'll tell you if you're going to be successful in life. Every second counts; we don't have much time. The clock ticks and the older we become, the less time we have left.

If you're a prisoner of fear, break free and become a prisoner of hope. Remember: if you don't stand for something, you will always fall for anything. Start by being part of something in your life. If you achieve it, it will mean so much to you and your family and friends. If you think life is hard, everything else will be difficult. If you realize the beauty of life and the freedom you have to determine your future, you'll find everything easy. Always work smart, not hard. Hard work is killing many dreams in our society today. Find some ways to spend time earning some sort of benefit. Avoid spending unnecessary, prolonged time on TV, video games, internet, etc that will yield you nothing. Life is too short to spend it on unproductive activities. Work now and play later, or play now and work later. Either way, it's your choice. If you have a full-time job, make it a habit to do something productive with your weekends and week nights. This will increase your chances of having more when you get older. Spending hours watching TVs and other unproductive activities will surely damage not only your dreams, but also your brain. Engage yourself in daily reading habits. Your mind needs to be aware of the progress in our community and society, both positive and negative. Always strive to be an example to others in your community, society, and family. It's time to posses your dream, to take faith over fear, and to expect favour in your future. Follow your dreams and the promises that God has given you.

Because most people believe success is impossible, they've stopped trying. Some think that success comes from luck, so they sit and wait for it. What you do now will determine your success. How your today impacts your tomorrow is the question you should be asking right now. We over-exaggerate our past and over-estimate our future, but the reality is that today is the long-awaited tomorrow we worried about yesterday. We also tend to under-estimate today. What have we accomplished today that will determine our tomorrow? Today is the most important day of your life. This moment is a blessing from God. Embrace and practice good nutrition, values, attitudes, and good thinking; seek, knock, ask, and experience great improvement in your life. Practice and exercise. Build concrete and lasting relationships. Give and support families, the needy, friends, and communities. If you manage like this, in addition to the positive attitude you already have, you'll be successful in life. Life is a journey, not a destination. Worries and regrets look backwards, but faith and hope look forward. Be passionate for passion. We are all uniquely made, but we all have one thing in common: the desire to get and feel what we want. Instead of tracing your problems around, start solving them. If you act the way you feel, soon you'll start feeling the way you act. We are winners in life; we therefore look to the future. Only the loser looks at the past and lives in regrets and pains. I believe we have a target now for everything we do and want to be in life, and we will be exactly what is it we want to be.

I am blessed to be a blessing. I believe that, with all my struggles and strengths, this is the most important service I could render to my community.

SECTION: WHY CHILD SOLDIER?

1. Why are child soldiers used?

They're cheap, malleable, they obey orders, and they don't have the same fears as adults. Experts say that children, who are eager to please and may not have developed a sense of right and wrong yet, are relatively easy to condition into obedient killing machines. And as conflicts drag on for years, a shortage of manpower may compel unscrupulous leaders to look to children to fill the ranks. These children are empty, they can be filled with whatever information you feed them with and most especially in the war setting, you do or die is mostly the case.

Francis Duworko

2. What is the role of child soldiers in Liberia?

Children have been an integral part of both government and rebel armies in Liberia since the country's thirteen-year civil war in the 1990s. In the recent conflict, which began in 2000, all three main factions--the government and rebel groups Liberians United for Reconciliation and Democracy (LURD) and Movement for Democracy in Liberia (MODEL)--used child soldiers. Former president Charles Taylor, who stepped down from office on August 11, 2003, recruited children into his National Patriotic Front of Liberia (NPFL) movement against the government of Samuel Doe in the late 1980s. He even formed a special brigade for them in his rebel army called the Small Boys Unit. This unit was one of the worst formed groups in the Liberian Civil war, because they had no limit, no fear and had big daddy's support.

3. How many where they?

Estimates in Liberia range from five to

fifteen thousand, with a huge escalation in the last couple of years, but there's no way to know for sure. Child soldiers could make up 25 to 75% of the total fighting forces in Liberia. Wikipedia states that, Worldwide, the United Nations estimates at least 300,000 children are used as combatants in war, with the greatest number in Burma, where there are some 70,000 child soldiers. Realistically, there were more child soldiers in Liberia and Sierra Leone than one can anticipate, but the main issue here is that the United Nations uses estimates for record's sake. I know because I was once.

4. Why do the children fight?

Many were forced to, and comply out of fear for their own lives. Some are seeking revenge against groups that killed their families, or a way to escape poverty. Many are drugged, with everything from liquor and marijuana to gun powder mixed into milk or cocaine rubbed into cuts on their faces. There were instances where children were forced to kill their parents and rape their sisters and relatives.

In so doing, they will be deadly, because if they didn't spare their own family whom shall they spare?

5. Are child soldiers involved in serious fighting?

Yes. Children in Liberia and neighboring Sierra Leone, where Taylor also supported armed rebel groups, have reported witnessing and participating in rapes, murders, executions, and the dismemberment and burning alive of victims. Many of them saw their loved ones killed in front of them, or were kidnapped and threatened with death if they didn't join in on the violence.

6. What kind of weapons are they using?

They use light, modern automatic weapons, including AK-47s and M-16s, G-3, Berriter, 50 Caliber, that are simple to operate and easily accessible in war-torn regions. Technological advances have made these and other weapons easy to strip, reassemble and fire, sending a steady stream of bullets with one pull of the trigger. Children also serve as human mine detectors, participate in suicide missions, and act as spies, messengers, or lookouts. Since children are considered less valuable than adult soldiers, they are often sent on very dangerous or suicidal missions. People have been considering children as less important in war, crisis, or violent situations, but in the war setting where children are been recruited as child soldiers, they can be very important because they don't have second thoughts. They operate on one instant feeling: we kill or we get killed. Sometimes they act out of fear of being killed.

7. Can they be reunited with their families?

In Liberia, family tracing is very, very important. As the conflict ended, the Red Cross set up a family reunification program that seeks to restore the child to his or her parents or extended family. In fact, in recent years since the Liberian civil war ended, many families have been reunited with their children. But taking back a child who's been through hell isn't easy. There are lots of challenges, especially if the child was with an armed group and killed people or committed atrocities. That might be hard for a family to accept. Some groups perform traditional reconciliation or forgiveness ceremonies, or ritual purification right, to help the child readjust to normal life. I think the widely-known fact that most children were taken against their will could help families accept them back. The challenge with ex-child soldiers reuniting with their families or communities over the years have been the past memories. Once on the wrong side of the family and friends, they're now coming back with nothing and expecting everything. It's really hard to accept, and these wounds on both sides will take time to heal, sometimes people point fingers. "He was one of them", and other times they're accused of atrocities.

AFRICAN NATIONS ACTION AGAINST CHILDREN SOLDIER AND UPDATES.

"The Cape Town Principles and Best Practices, adopted by the NGO Working Group on the Convention on the Rights of Children and UNICEF at a symposium on the prevention of recruitment of children into the armed forces, and on demobilization and social regeneration of child soldiers in Africa in April 1997, proposed that African governments should adopt and ratify the Optional protocol on the involvement of children in armed conflict raising the minimum age from 15 to 18, and that African Governments should ratify and implement other pertinent treaties and incorporate them into national law. The symposium defined a child soldier as any person under age 18 who is "part of any kind of regular or irregular armed force or group in any capacity, including but not limited to cooks, porters, messengers and those accompanying such groups, other than purely as family members." (Wikipedia) The definition includes girls recruited for sexual purposes and for forced marriage. It does not, therefore, only refer to a child who is carrying or has carried arms. (WIKIPEDIA)

Up to half of the world's child soldiers are in Africa (according to UNOCHA) in 2004, one estimate put the number of children involved in armed conflict including combat roles at 100,000, In the end titles of the film Blood Diamond, it is claimed that "there are still 200,000 child soldiers in Africa"(internet Wikipedia). Many of these children are "invisible children," orphaned by AIDS, violence and war. These children are as young as 7 years old and are forced into conflict due to poverty, sold by their parents, kidnapped, or tricked into joining. (According to UNOCHA) These children are our future leaders and they've been taught the wrong things and the wrong ways of life" (internet Wikipedia).

SECTION: LIFE

You may have been thinking;

Life is a goal, achieve it...always define who you want to be in life and be it.

Life is a challenge, meet it...anything that's worth fighting for is worth the price.

Life is a gift, accept it...life is given to us once and we don't have a second chance, we live it once and for all. It's a gift not a right.

Life is an adventure, dare it...life is living every possibility that defines you. Live it to the fullest.

Life is a sorrow, overcome it...life is full of surprises, keep faith in everything you do in good or bad times.

Life is a tragedy, face it...every day is not Christmas. Expect rainy days to come your way at times.

Life is a game, play it...there are two sides to life, you are either a winner or a looser, you can't be both at the same time.

Life is a mystery, unfold it...you can be whatever you choose to be or at least you can keep trying to solve the puzzle of life, failure is not a disgrace

Life is a song sing it...speaks positively about your living situation, if you are down and you want to get back up, prophesy your future positively.

Life is an opportunity, take it...opportunity comes every moment as we breathe, always take advantage of them when they show up.

Life is a promise fulfill it...we are to live life to the fullest

Life is love, enjoy it...enjoy every breath

Life is a beauty, praise it...it's good to have all the good things life has to offer

Life is a spirit, realize it...realize that you are living life, this is it...

Life is a puzzle, solve it...like red banana, you can't tell where exactly it will break until it breaks

Life is worth living, live it to the fullest and you shall lack nothing

There are many children on the streets of most African, American, and Canadian cities that deserve the right to a mother and father, and to education, food and shelter. Due to crisis and war situations in their communities and countries, their rights are being abused, and these experiences grow with them into adulthood, causing our world to go bad. I'm not talking about uncontrolled situations, like the pre-mature death of a partner, but situations we human beings can control; such as getting a divorce, having an unwanted pregnancy, making wrongful decisions for our family, etc. Countries like Liberia, Sierra Leone, Guinea, Ivory Coast, Sudan, Libya, and so many others that have had terrible experiences as a result of conflicts, crisis, and war are still suffering from the effects of the past, leading their children and youths onto the streets, making the country unsafe for mankind to survive. If there is no immediate intervention, our world will soon become a land of savage thieves and cruel leaders who will play corrupt roles in our society. I think it is high time we started paying closer attention to what and how we want our world to look like in the future, and the best way to do this is by paying close attention on our children and what we want them to be. Every child should have equal opportunities in life, despite their physical, emotional, cultural, ethnic, status or financial background. If this is true for all children, what will life be like for a child who has missed out on all of these rights, and has grown with so much hatred, anger, and pain as an ex-child soldier in this world. I also pray for our planet to keep bringing forth great people who will continue making this world a better place to live by standing and fighting for the rights of their children.

Many of us struggle with the reality that yesterday is gone and we are not to worry about it. All it has is pains, frustrations, hurts, disappointments, regrets, discomforts and unhappiness. If we're always looking backwards to the past, we're in the repairing mode. This is a waste of time; we will live our entire lives trying to pay for the mistakes and ignorance of the past. If we always look forward to the future by doing the best we can today, we prepare the future. This is the correct mood to be in. Yesterday is gone forever with its drama; we have no control over tomorrow, and all we have now is today. Believing and living today will take us on a journey to a reality where we can do or be anything we want. Always pay the price; taking the free ride in your own life will make other people achieve their dreams, leaving us with nothing. Remember to work hard to achieve your dreams.

I don't remember a lot from my childhood, for the experiences in the war have damaged my ability to recall. I consider myself tough because I cannot be broken easily, base on my past experiences. There have been tough times in my life that I wouldn't wish anyone to go through, but I did survive them. To experience means to have faced the challenge and either overcome it or have it overcome you. In either case, be sure to live to tell. Making it to this point was simple. Today is the most significant event of my life, and I have always known that I would survive to see it.

My coming to Canada was a bit challenging, because upon arrival my brother took ill, and was diagnosed with cancer. It was so severe that he underwent seven different operations, including two major operations in six months before getting rid of the tumour. I was devastated and disappointed. I came to Canada with many expectations, just like many immigrants, but this was not one of them. Today has been the main tool in my life. I am leaving you with the challenge of making it your main tool. Live in the present only; let's do our best for today. Tomorrow will become today in a matter of hours, and yesterday is just a word. It means nothing, so it should have no hold on us. It takes a kind heart to help others in desperate situations. These stories and experiences happened to me because it was destined. Through them, I've become an expert in helping others overcome similar challenges in life. I like to imitate good people in my community. They made it, and we can all make it through their examples of leadership skills. I believe in people who believe in themselves. I love to help people make changes, especially those who want to make a huge impact on many lives.

END